Coffee Connections

FINDING COMMON GROUND
THROUGH MY DAILY BREW

Coffee Connections

FINDING COMMON GROUND THROUGH MY DAILY BREW

Wendy Bornstein

BELLA COSE

Boston, Massachusetts

BELLA COSE

Contact publisher at www.Wendy-Bornstein.com

Paperback: 978-1-7374086-1-1
Mobi: 978-1-7374086-2-8
EPUB: 978-1-7374086-3-5
LCCN: 2021911907
Library of Congress cataloging in publication data on file with the publisher.

Publishing, Production & Marketing:
Concierge Marketing, Inc.
www.ConciergeMarketing.com

Printed in the United States
10 9 8 7 6 5 4

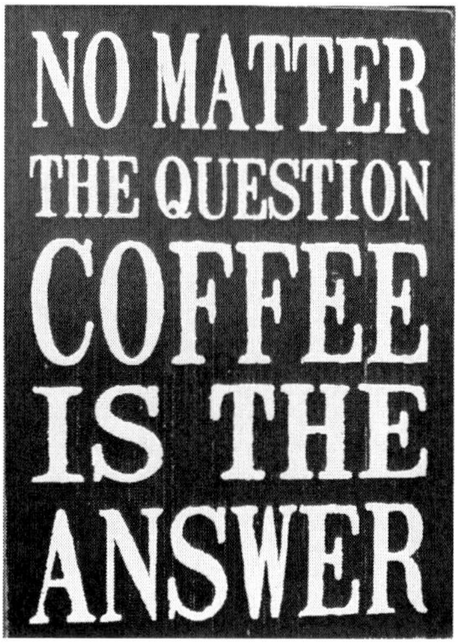

NO MATTER
THE QUESTION
COFFEE
IS THE
ANSWER

This book is dedicated to the eternal memories of my parents, Herb and Audrey Stearns. I also share reflections of other relatives throughout this book and look forward to creating new memories each and every day to be shared with future generations.

I love coffee. In fact, I have often been accused of loving coffee more than my husband. Coffee is my lifeline, and there are times when I can't function without a caffeine infusion. That being said, coffee runs through my veins and is a part of me. I concur with **The National Coffee Association USA's** statement about coffee:

We believe that coffee is more than just a drink: It's a culture, an economy, an art, a science—and a passion. Whether you're new to the brew or an espresso expert, there's always more to learn about this beloved beverage.[1]

In this book I will share how coffee has connected me to life beyond the cup.

Contents

Part 1:
The Beginnings

Part Two: Married with Kids

Part Three:
Nest Starting to Empty

Part Four:
Empty Nest Syndrome

Part Five:
2020—The New Normal of "Covid Coffee"

Foreword

"Every opportunity starts as a conversation."

Wendy's path through life was not predictable—and behind every move and kid and dog and job and friend and house we find her one true and constant love. Her confidante and comforter. Her sounding board and soother. Her pick-me-up and proving ground.

"Her husband," you're probably thinking.

And you're wrong.

It's coffee.

Conversations over coffee strengthened and sustained her through several careers, kids, pets, and community involvement. Coffee informs where she travels and how she starts her day. Coffee has brought her friends, clients, and opportunities.

This book is a fun and touching and sweet and engaging tour of the various stages of Wendy's life, told from the perspective of her coffee conversations.

I enjoy teaching people how to do this—how to sit down and get to know people in a way that creates opportunities on both sides. It's an honor and a joy to introduce the book of someone who has truly mastered the art of getting to know people.

Her story is a true testament to the power of conversations in guiding our lives and work.

May it inspire you, as it has me, to keep starting better conversations!

Andrew Winig

Elevator Pitch Coach and author of the *Elevator Pitch Handbook*

ImprovAndy.com

Preface

Dear Bruce,

When we married, I vowed to honor and obey you through sickness and in health. I now have to confess that I have had a long-term relationship that started before we met and continues to this day. I think it is time to share this with you.

My other relationship began several years before we met and has lasted ever since. There is not a day that goes by that I don't lust for it. The desire is a constant in my soul. It gives me energy and focus. Without it I cannot function.

This other love is my affinity for coffee. It has become an integral part of my daily routine. I look forward to a morning cup as soon as I crawl out of bed.

Before I start telling this story, I want to preface by saying that I realize you are not a coffee drinker. For me, there is a *purpose behind every cup of coffee I drink. This is a key differ-ence between us. You drink coffee to stay awake, while I drink coffee to enjoy the experience. At the end of a day it is often a long-anticipated treat. In the pages that follow, I will elaborate in more detail.*

I hope that reading this book will help you understand my lifelong affair with coffee. I will start at the beginning…

With love,

Wendy

Introduction

I started drinking coffee when I was a preteen living with my parents in Newton, Massachusetts. Throughout my forty-plus years of daily brews I have gone to college, lived in Connecticut and New York as a single person, moved back to Boston, married my husband Bruce, raised our three children, Gregory, Rachael, and Michelle, and adopted our Havanese dog, Delilah.

Over this time period I have been a child, college student, yuppie, wife, parent, caretaker for elderly parents, and now a baby boomer and empty nester.

Simultaneously I have been a renter and homeowner while transitioning between various careers. I started in the corporate business world, transitioned to become an independent consultant and then a professional volunteer during and beyond the kids' school years before moving into my current career as a Realtor. The one consistency in my daily routine has been a morning coffee.

In this book I will share some of the insights and experiences I have had while going through each phase of my life cycle. During the COVID-19 Stay at Home period in particular, I have had time to reminisce and travel back through my memory bank. I have tried to go in chronological order as much as possible; however, certain segments of my journey may span a wider time gap. I had talked about writing this book for the past ten years, and I guess one gift of the pandemic has been finally having the time to start.

I invite you to grab a cup of coffee and share my journey!

Part 1:
The Beginnings

Sometime Around 1970

My connection with coffee began at a young age. I was not much of a milk drinker as a child and particularly hated plain milk. My mom always tried to encourage us to drink more milk because she thought it was important to have calcium in our diet. My dislike for milk began when I drank from a sour-tasting Hood's milk carton during a bus ride to day camp.

Since I refused to drink milk, Mom tried all kinds of strategies to get me to have calcium. I was always weight conscious and believed the old wives' tale that chocolate caused acne. Thus, I avoided Nestle's Quik and Hershey's syrup at all costs. As a last resort, she introduced me to coffee when I was about age eleven by giving me a glass of half milk and half coffee. I agreed to drink milk this way and started to acquire a taste for the beverage. Although I didn't love it at first, I drank it regularly to satisfy nutritional guidelines. The more I had, the more I began to like the taste, and gradually I changed the ratios to include more coffee and less milk. I continued to drink it this way until starting college.

Wendy 1970

Of note: My mom had her "Maxwell House" coffee every morning while she read the newspaper. My younger brother is named Maxwell, and although he was named after my father's father, I always thought there was an ulterior motive in choosing his name. (On a weird side note, during the Jewish holiday of Passover, Maxwell House Coffee offered a free Haggadah with each one-pound purchase of coffee, and this was the Haggadah of choice for our family. We owned several of these.)[2]

Growing up, I remember Mom, Grandma Sarah (Ring), and Aunt Elaine (Wolpe) sitting around the kitchen table and chatting over coffee. Sometimes my great-grandmother, Bubbe Rachael (Piltch), would join them, although she was a tea drinker. They talked about family and the kids. They also talked about my aunt's travels, the latest fashions, and books they had read. Aunt Elaine, who lived in Pennsylvania, was an avid reader. She also traveled a lot with my uncle who was a Rabbi and would often bring me something from her latest venture. She would visit with her four sons and my uncle every summer and occasionally during the year. When possible, she would stop by the Boston area en route to one of her travel destinations. She was a role model for me, and I always looked forward to these visits. From her, I developed the quest for travel, the art of shopping, and the love of reading.

After a round of morning coffee, we would head out for a shopping venture (of note, I was the only girl on both sides of my immediate family, which sometimes gave me shopping privileges) to Loehman's and Hoffman's in Natick and always end the day with a stop at Eagerman's Bakery on Route 9 to buy bagels and bupke (Jewish coffee cake) to enjoy the next morning with coffee. We would also stop for lunch, where they always ordered coffee with grilled cheese or tuna sandwiches. As I reflect now, I was excited to be invited to join the "coffee club," although I was only halfway there until a bit later. The concept of being a coffee drinker was ingrained in my blood.

In high school I read *Coffee, Tea or Me?* by Trudy Baker[3]. The book chronicled the experiences of two flight attendants, and although the focus was on passengers being more interested in the "Me," I became obsessed with the "Coffee." In addition, I was intrigued by the flight attendants' opportunities for travel. After reading the book, I made a one-dollar bet with my brother Max that I would become a flight attendant after college. To this day I have not fulfilled my end of the bet and pray he does not expect the royalties from this book.

Family legacy photo with grandparents

1976-1980: The College Years and Stayin' Alive

At college I was introduced to the concept of using caffeine as a stimulant to stay awake during study periods. [I studied at the University of Massachusetts (UMASS) for my undergraduate degree in Business.] This benefit would become the impetus for my lifelong coffee indulgence. I watched my peers as they headed for the Campus Center Coffee Shop between classes. After having a hard time staying awake during first period classes I would join them for a coffee break. The coffee was pretty bad, but I soon discovered that their one-dollar six-inch chocolate chip cookies paired well enough to make it tolerable. I drank coffee in college mostly to stay awake, and it became my "go to" drink whenever I had to pull all-nighters to study for exams. There were a few local coffee shops that had better coffee, but the Campus Center was the most convenient.

The late '70s brought the rise of disco and going to clubs. *Saturday Night Fever*[4] was the number one movie, and it provided many of the songs played through the nights of partying. A favorite of mine was "Stayin' Alive," and I even took a disco dancing one-credit course so I could learn the moves for Thursday night visits to "Poor Richard's Pub."

In addition to keeping us awake to study, coffee helped us recover from hangovers. Coffee was not served in the library; thus, students would trek to the Campus Center for a quick break. It was rare to see friends and fellow students focus social gatherings around coffee. Socialization was saved for post-study time when homework was finished and we could go to the local bars or frat keg parties. In the late '70s the legal drinking age was 18, which meant that we could gather publicly to drink alcohol.

The year before I graduated from college (1979) the drinking age was raised to 20 in Massachusetts[5], and by 1984 it was raised nationwide to age 21 under President Reagan[6]. The implications of these changes would lay the foundation for an emerging coffee market in America.

Around this time, a new trend favoring high-end, fresh-brewed coffee was beginning to emerge in the Boston area. George Howell introduced the foundation of coffee culture to Boston in 1975 with his insight into the popularity of good brews coming from the West Coast, particularly Seattle, Washington. He opened a coffee shop in Cambridge named The Coffee Connection[7]. Next, Howell opened a shop in Newton where I had grown up. Eventually Coffee Connection locations also opened in Brookline, Wellesley, and a few other suburbs. These became perfect destination venues for students to meet friends when they were home on college breaks.

Since I was already over age 21 by the time Reagan's act became law, it didn't have as much impact on me as it did on my younger brother and future generations of college students. Recognizing that Boston was a major college hub, it made sense that coffee shops like the Coffee Connection would flourish in the metropolitan area. Where else could students legally gather to chat and socialize, particularly during daytime hours?

Before long coffee shops became a place to study, see peers, arrange weekend dates, make travel plans, and potentially meet someone for an interview or even a first date. The local coffee shop served as a platform for a quick meeting or a gateway to future engagement. In Brookline, a place called Bagel Nosh[8] became a "hot spot" to catch up with friends after a date and compare notes while waiting in line for a bagel and coffee.

15

1980–1982: On-the-Job Training

First Stop: Connecticut

Upon college graduation my relationship with coffee became more serious. Although I decided to pursue a career in finance instead of becoming a flight attendant, I still had a burning desire to travel.

My first real job after college was with Emhart Corporation, a Fortune 500 manufacturing company based in Farmington, Connecticut, a suburb a few miles west of Hartford. I was hired as an internal auditor. A main appeal of the job would be the opportunity to travel to corporate subsidiaries. While I was growing up, my travel had been limited primarily to the northeastern United States and Quebec. I was ripe to explore the world.

In this role, I would conduct onsite audits of Emhart Manufacturing subsidiaries in Connecticut and other states. My first assignments included a six-week trip to Tampa, Florida, and a twelve-week assignment in Torrance, California.

I was often the only female on the assignment, accompanied by three or four male colleagues. On the road they would go to clubs to meet women and drink. On one such visit to Tampa they were going to a table dancing strip club. I had no idea what it was and naively joined them. Feeling very uncomfortable, I left early and took a cab back to the hotel. After that night, I spent much of my future travel time watching TV alone in my hotel room.

On a subsequent assignment we drove from California to Las Vegas for a weekend field trip. This was my first time in Las Vegas, and again, I had no idea what to expect. As it turned out, I didn't see my colleagues again until it was time to head back to Torrance. As I listened to their conversations in the car (since they didn't adhere to *"what happens in Vegas stays in Vegas"*), I was glad I hadn't seen them all weekend. While I was in Vegas, I had ended up going to dinner and seeing Wayne Newton by myself.

The audit department was predominantly made up of toxic males. At Emhart's headquarters, the office coffee maker was where the boys' club would gather to talk sports and compare their notes about the women they had scored with on their road trips. Since I had little interest in either topic, this was not a comfortable job environment.

One time when I was walking by the coffee room, I overheard my supervisor Rick share some crude comments about a female colleague that brought snickers from his listeners. After I had spent six months at Emhart, I learned that my direct manager Jeff had been let go for "a harassment issue" and that Rick would now be running the department.

Unhappy with this change, I decided to pursue new job options. My dad told me I had to stay with a job at least a year or it would hurt my résumé. I had started at Emhart on August 1, 1980, and I gave my notice effective August 1, 1981.

I did not like Hartford at that stage of my life. It was not a good fit for young single women craving a social life. In fact, the extent of my Hartford social life consisted of visits from friends who needed a rest stop between Boston and New York. I also learned that I did not like the manufacturing industry and did not fit in with "the boys' club."

Next Up: New York

I began researching more service-oriented companies, with a top priority being employers with a more equal balance between males and females. I had always aspired to live in New York City, so I focused my search there. I took the Frank Sinatra song "New York, New York"[9] to heart, and it became my mantra. I told my friends that Hartford had just been a stop along the way.

My dad arranged for me to speak with a headhunter he had met while working for Panasonic in Secaucus, New Jersey. After interviewing with several companies, I landed an internal audit position with Dun & Bradstreet Corporation (D&B) in 1982 and was excited to move to NYC.

In my new job, I became part of a group of about 20 to 30 auditors, both male and female and all close to my age. I would still be able to travel and explore the world, but this time I would have peers who would join me as a tourist as we traveled together domestically and abroad.

Working for D&B was a great opportunity for me. I found an apartment in Forest Hills in the borough of Queens and took the E or F Train to the Citicorp Building. Every morning

I would walk up Lexington Avenue and hustle down East 52nd Street to D&B's headquarters at 299 Park Avenue.

My office was on a high floor somewhere above the 20th. I learned that the Corporate Executives were on the 9th floor. Employees at my staff level were not allowed to visit the 9th floor. There was a defined corporate hierarchy of who could talk with whom. I observed that my colleagues always carried a cup of take-out coffee with them as they entered the elevator and would be rather quiet until we passed the 9th floor.

During the '80s in New York it was common to go to **Chock Full o' Nuts** or a little deli shop where take-out cups always had the classic Greek design. After a commute on the train to the city, everyone would typically grab a take-out cup and then run to their workplace, panting because the line had taken longer than expected. Wanting to fit in with my peers, I decided "when in New York, act like a New Yorker." I began to wear sneakers during the commute and do like the locals. Thus began my daily first cup.

Greek mug

My primary responsibility as an auditor was to conduct due diligence on various departments within the Company to assure that they were complying with SEC guidelines in their accounting and business practices (in Europe and Canada, these were U.S. subsidiaries). This role could be seen as adversarial if it was not handled correctly. The position involved extensive travel, and I would often be away for weeks at a time.

I was very excited to be able to travel on a company-paid expense account. On weekends we would have the option to return home if domestic or enjoy personal travel if the cost was comparable. I took full advantage of this unique opportunity and explored as much as I could after work hours. Many of my peers were seasoned travelers and less enthusiastic than I was about traveling.

I eventually learned that business travel can become old, but initially I was thrilled at the prospect. I developed an insatiable desire to learn as much as I could about different cultures and places before visiting each destination. I wanted to take full advantage of each travel opportunity. Back in the '80s we did not have as many resources as we do today, so I had to rely mostly on AAA or similar travel guidebooks as well as others' personal stories.

In my role as an auditor, it was important to build a rapport with the client before interviewing them about business-related issues. I soon discovered that chatting over a cup of coffee with the office staff was a great ice-breaker and a good way to learn the basics of the area. I would often start by asking about favorite foods and local sightseeing destinations. I quickly discovered how much people love to open up and share information if you ask the right questions.

Having a cup of coffee with clients seemed to transcend international boundaries and begin building trust, thus opening a door to better delve into the tasks at hand for the particular assignment. My travels took me to Montreal, Toronto, Vancouver, the UK, Rotterdam, and many U.S. states. During this stage of my career in the early '80s I learned that offering someone a cup of coffee was one of the best introductory tools to begin engagement and initiate conversation.

Landing in London

On one of my first Dun & Bradstreet audit assignments I met a woman in the UK office who would become a good friend during the six weeks I spent in London. Although she typically drank tea, knowing I was American she offered me a cup of coffee at our first meeting. At this encounter she shared her insights on London from a local perspective, including advice on places to safely take a morning run, where to shop, and other things one would not know as a tourist.

For example, she suggested I visit the Marks & Spencer store in the early morning to buy clothing basics and underwear. At that time they sold apparel that was well made and reasonably priced. She said this was where she shopped. The timing of my visit was soon after the Royal Wedding of Lady Diana Spencer and Prince Charles. Coincidentally, Lady Diana was part of the Marks & Spencer family.

During my visit, I was introduced to the "British" way of drinking tea with a drop of milk. The coffee in the UK wasn't great, and I ended up drinking primarily tea during this visit. However, drinking tea with my new friends reinforced the value of talking as a means of building rapport and establishing a longer-term relationship. As a departure gift from the London visit, my friend gave me a beer stein with gold trim and the insignia of the Royal Wedding. To this day I attribute our friendship to the initial cup of coffee we shared.

Back to New York

While I was working for D&B I traveled about 75 percent of the time and spent the rest of my time in New York. When I was in the NYC office, I began to notice that my colleagues would congregate around the coffee pot to take five-minute breaks throughout the day. After a few weeks at the office, I started to follow suit. At first I talked mostly with my colleagues, but then I realized that these breaks offered opportunities to meet other department staffers as well. I began to befriend the habitual regulars, whom I learned had a predetermined daily schedule. Soon I developed FOMO (fear of missing out) if I had to skip a break.

Most of my colleagues went out after work for drinks when they were in town. They enjoyed the hard liquor beverages at bars around Lexington and 52nd Street, such as **Gallagher's** and the **Belfry**. This was out of my budget, and honestly the prospect of drinking alcohol at a bar did little to make me justify an after-work cocktail. I was still a bit traumatized remembering my Emhart experience and was very cautious about reliving it again.

While I was home for an eight-week project I developed a first crush on someone I met over coffee at the office. It started when an Internal Audit Department friend told me that Kevin from Accounting wanted to meet me. Kevin would grab a coffee at 10:00 a.m. every morning, so I started to do the same. After a few weeks of flirtation, he asked me out for dinner. We ended up dating, but our relationship didn't last long. After we broke up, I felt awkward getting coffee in the office and started to go outside for my caffeine fix.

During my time at D&B, I became very good friends with a few colleagues in my department. Two of these friends, Robin and Dawn, were a year or two ahead of me and facing promotions. Dawn was tired of the travel and ended up leaving the job to get married and settle down. Robin was a workaholic type and lived for work. She had recently been promoted to Supervisor level, and the guys on her team were not too happy about her new position. I think they felt threatened by a female in a position of authority, as most supervisors were male at this time. After hearing mixed stories, I became nervous when I was assigned to work on a local audit with Robin as the lead supervisor.

I decided to try my coffee technique with Robin to get to know her beyond her work image and suggested we go out for lunch sometime. She never took breaks during the day but instead suggested we go out after work to grab a coffee at Zabars near Grand Central Station or the Citicorp building before heading home on our respective trains.

Although I felt intimidated at first, I was able to get Robin to open up and share a bit about her background. Over coffee she told me about her career aspirations and mentioned that she was an only child. She had the stereotypical heavy Long Island accent and attitude, but my impression of Robin changed as I got to know her. Her parents had divorced when she was young, and she was driven to achieve financial independence at all costs. She was very Type A and had to be in control of her environment. I gained insight into the motivation behind her domineering personality, and we were able to work well together. We soon developed a friendship outside of work boundaries and enjoyed theater and coffee get-togethers on a regular basis.

During my time at D&B I learned that the best way to work with people was to find common ground. Over the course of a drink, people are more prone to open up to conversation. For many of the men this meant going to a bar to grab a beer or hard liquor. The women seemed to enjoy more intimate conversation over a cup of coffee or tea.

1982-1984: Rerouting My Roots

To this day I continue to use the skills I developed at D&B whenever I meet with a potential real estate client or begin a new project with colleagues. I have found that the enjoyment of a cup of coffee is a common thread among my friends and associates. Accordingly, I always offer coffee to anyone crossing my home threshold, whether it be a visiting guest or a contractor coming to perform work at my house. I consider this a chance to welcome each individual and express gratitude for the anticipated interaction.

When I traveled to Canada and Amsterdam for D&B, coffee shops were popular gathering places. In London, the focus was on socializing at pubs after work and at tea during the day. I never quite acquired a taste for beer, but I did try tea and crumpets a few times.

Whenever I spent time away from home, I missed my family and friends. This was long before the advent of email and cell phones. It was always a pleasure to head back to Boston and see my parents after returning from work-related travels. I became obsessed with good coffee and started dragging my parents to the **Coffee Connection (CC)** when I came home for a weekend visit.

Does Father Know Best?

On one visit in particular, I remember my dad picking me up at Logan Airport at noon and spending more than an hour talking with me at the CC in Coolidge Corner to catch up on life. My mom was very busy getting the house ready for Passover and insisted that Dad pick me up. He agreed to do so if we could stop for candy at Waldman's Candy Store on Harvard Street in Brookline.

Dad had certain topics of interest to talk to me about before I spoke with Mom, such as his ideas about who I should date or career advice he wanted to share with me. He relished the time he could spend alone with me over a cup of coffee. He only had an undergraduate degree in Liberal Arts from Boston University and thought it was vital for me to get an MBA.

I knew that Dad hated the corporate business world. He often cited the challenges he faced as a salesperson and wanted me to do "better" by acquiring management skills. He would always cite *The Peter Principle*[10], which ultimately suggested that employees were constantly promoted until they rose to a level of incompetence. He felt it became harder and harder to live up to the next level of expectation with each promotion.

As a child I sometimes accompanied Dad on day trips to visit his clients. He was a manufacturer's representative for Panasonic, and his market was Mom & Pop stores in the 1960s and '70s. The retail industry was beginning to shift from small, local, independent shops to big chain stores with corporate headquarters out of state. Dad didn't adapt well to this change, and sadly, neither did his client base who found it hard to compete with the volume of the big-box retailers. The sales skills and rapport he had built over the years at the local level was becoming obsolete, and success was measured only by dollar volume. He eventually left the corporate sales world. He urged me to get an MBA so I could compete at the top of my game.

Since these visits took place well before the advent of cell phones, my mom was extremely worried about our long trip home and would yell, "Where were you?" when we walked into the house after our "very long" ride home from the airport.

My dad's advice was very sound, and I heeded it in later years. As I reflect on these little coffee talks, I have a renewed appreciation for the lasting impact my dad has had on my life. By observing his ability to build rapport with clients, I learned techniques that were ingrained in me at an early age.

Falling, Falling… Fell, and My Aunt Knew, Too?

Another weekend visit home would become significant for another reason. During this trip in spring 1983, my longtime friend Bruce stopped by my parents' house to see me. We went out (I like to think it was for coffee, but he said it was for ice cream). He was just finishing the last year of Medical School and would soon be starting his internship at Mt. Auburn Hospital. For some unexplainable reason, I found his conversation more interesting than I had during his prior visits.

27

Bruce and I had been good friends since high school. When we met, he was about to start his undergraduate degree at MIT, and I had just completed my junior year of high school. Bruce had grown up less than two miles from me in Needham. Throughout the course of my college years and work travels, I would always make time to meet him for a quick bite or ice cream when I was in town to see my parents. I was not yet ready to pursue a boyfriend-girlfriend relationship during these get-togethers. After each visit, he would say that he would wait for me. I would often shrug off this comment, knowing he really "liked" me. In fact, one time before this visit in 1983, I remember Aunt Elaine saying, "Wouldn't it be funny if you ended up with THAT Bruce Bornstein someday." Well, I soon learned that my aunt was always right.

Wendy and Bruce, 1983

Part Two:
Married with Kids

1984-1989: Homeward Bound

I stayed at D&B for two years and soon began to miss my life back in Boston. Traveling for work was no longer so exciting, and I developed a bad case of FOMO (fear of missing out) from my friends in Boston whenever I got a message on my answering machine that "so and so" was engaged. My 75% travel was too much, and I began to seek opportunities beyond the world of Internal Auditing.

I met with Robin a few times for coffee after work hours, as she recently had experienced similar feelings and moved to a role in a subsidiary. She was not overly thrilled about her new position, and this further motivated me to begin looking for opportunities both internally and outside the company. Around this time, I also had started to date my now-husband, Bruce.

On a subsequent visit home, I went out for coffee with my dad and shared my new interest in Bruce. Dad gave me the "seal of approval" and his blessings. This time, my mom expected us to take a longer than normal ride home from the airport.

When I was back in NYC I informed Robin of my interest in Bruce and my desire to move back to Boston. An additional motivation for this move was the fact that my Grandmother Sarah, who had been stricken with breast cancer, was in remission and I longed to be closer to her. I was ready to return to my hometown roots.

Robin asked me why I would ever want to leave the City. When I mentioned missing greenery and my family, she suggested that I could always visit a tree in Central Park. I started to send résumés to companies in the Boston area, and in the late spring of 1983 I was hired by Damon Corporation in Needham as a senior accountant. This new job involved minimal domestic travel. I followed my dad's advice and started applying to MBA programs. I also took his blessing as Bruce and I became serious and were soon engaged.

We were married in June of 1984 and celebrated our honeymoon with a week in Bermuda between Bruce's internship and residency. I enrolled in the evening MBA program at Boston University that fall. This was an opportune time for me to pursue postgraduate study, since Bruce would be working many weekends during his residency program. The combination of a full-time day job and evening classes was tiring, and it became habitual for me to get a large coffee before class. Fortunately, there was a coffee shop near the Sargent Business School.

In 1984 coffee culture was not yet big in Massachusetts except for the **Coffee Connection**. After getting married, Bruce and I found an apartment in Newtonville where we lived throughout Bruce's residency and my MBA program. Fortunately, there was a Coffee Connection near us, and I would often get takeout to bring with me during weekend study sessions at the Boston College library.

I left Damon after about three years and was hired in 1986 by McCormack and Dodge, a mainframe software company in Natick. I accepted a supervisory role in the finance department managing the budget process with minimal travel. M&D was a subsidiary of Dun & Bradstreet, and I was excited about this opportunity. An added bonus was that since I had previously worked for D&B, I was reinstated to the level of retirement plan vesting I had achieved while I was in NYC.

By the end of my second year at M&D, I was promoted to Finance Manager and reported directly to Director Level Senior Management. I was responsible for Strategic Planning and Finance.

During my third year at M&D I became pregnant with our first child, Greg. I took a pregnancy class at the JCC (Jewish Community Center) in Newton and saw someone there who looked familiar. It turned out that Joan, one of the attendees in the JCC course, was working in M&D's marketing department. We became instant friends. We both had developed cravings for pizza during our pregnancies and started frequenting Papa Gino's next door to our office. We also loved coffee and looked forward to the day when we could switch from decaf to regular post-pregnancy.

My son Greg and Joan's son Alexander were born within weeks of each other, and we started a playgroup with a few other moms from the JCC. Our weekly playdates were followed by coffee with the babies in tow at the JCC café. When the boys were less than a year old, M&D merged with a company in Atlanta, Georgia. I was offered the opportunity to relocate to Atlanta, but relocating was not in the cards at that time.

1990–1995: Baby Steps

After being laid off from my job at McCormack and Dodge, I had ample free time. I was also fortunate to receive a generous severance package, which gave me the opportunity to decide what to do next while still collecting a paycheck for a few months. Part of my severance included the chance to work with a career counselor to help figure out my next move. I was offered two career tracks: (1) try to find a similar position with another company, or (2) start my own business as a consultant.

Since Joan had also been laid off by M&D, we regularly set up playdates with our young sons. We would often meet at Joan's house in Newton Center and take Baby Gregory and her son Baby Alex for walks in Newton Center. We would always make a stop at the Coffee Connection and get takeout cups of coffee, walk, and then head to the playground. This was a great time to share ideas of what our next job roles might be. Joan also had a severance package and was interviewing at other software companies. These playdates became a routine thing, and my addiction to good coffee was firmly established.

Baby Alex and Baby Greg

Recalling my dad's advice about becoming my own boss, coupled with wanting to have a more flexible schedule while raising a young child, I opted for the second severance option: starting my own business as a consultant. I put together my résumé and was advised to conduct informational interviews with companies to find my niche. The career counselor encouraged me to arrange network meetings with any contacts I had as well as business leaders to figure out my future path. Meeting people for coffee was a good way to conduct market research, and I found myself making many new "coffee" connections. I also attended networking events through the BU alumni association.

During this time I started to attend some Small Business Administration (SBA) events and met a man who had just invested in a new company called Starbucks. He said they were a growing company from the West Coast and that they charged a dollar for a cup of coffee that cost them less than 10 cents to make. He thought it was a great investment and predicted that we would be hearing a lot about Starbucks in the near future.

Half Caf, Please

As the weather turned cooler and the boys started to do more indoor activities, Joan and I began venturing to the JCC or Gymboree in Newton and then McDonald's after class for Happy Meals. To keep the moms happy, too, we would first stop at the Coffee Connection. Diaper bags filled with coloring books, crayons, and eventually Gameboys kept the boys occupied as Joan and I enjoyed our coffee. These dates continued for about a year or so until Joan got a new job. I also started to do some consulting for a software company in Waltham, which lasted until I eventually gave birth to our second child. During this second pregnancy, I again switched to decaf.

Our daughter Rachael was born in 1991. After her birth, I continued to do some financial consulting on a limited part-time basis for local software companies. I went back to drinking coffee because I really needed the caffeine. With two kids and part-time work, I was on a constant treadmill for a few more years.

Sometime in late 1993 or early '94 (I can't remember exact dates), I heard that Starbucks was coming to Massachusetts and that they were taking over the **Coffee Connection** shops in Wellesley and Newton Center. I remembered my previous conversation at the networking event and was eager to check out Starbucks. I soon visited the Newton Center location while seeing my parents who still lived in Newton at the time.[11]

Perhaps it was the intrigue of the investor combined with the lure of romanticism that drew me to Starbucks. I had read a few novels during my layoff period and learned how aspiring authors spent much of their time in cafés to network while writing books. I later learned that café culture was a thing for Jews in Europe, so maybe it was in my genes to become a coffee connoisseur. I quickly became obsessed with Starbucks.[12]

During this period, I was frequently hired to work on short-term projects for consulting clients. Often a project would evolve to create a need for a full-time staff position. When I shared that I only wanted to work part-time, I would often find my role eliminated when the client hired a full-time equivalent. This continued for about three years as I embraced part-time work. Then, knowing I was expecting our third child, I went light on coffee during the pregnancy and revisited the half caf of my early years.

1994: Love at First Sight: A "Star"bucks Is Born

While I was cutting back on my caffeine intake during pregnancy in late 1994, Starbucks was gradually taking over all the Coffee Connections in Massachusetts. I was excited to learn they would be replacing a favorite family store, Calverts, in Needham Heights.

Michelle was born in 1995. After her birth I was eager to drink "real" coffee again. She and I would spend much of our time at the new Starbucks in Needham, as it was conveniently located near both sets of grandparents and en route to the JCC. Michelle tagged along with me each morning after we dropped Gregory and Rachael off at school. Raising three young kids was exhausting, and Starbucks became a frequent must-have stop.

Playgroups came and went during this time. I sometimes joined local Dover playgroups and also participated in one from the JCC. Michelle and I would take Gymboree-type classes there and then go to the Needham Starbucks for a snack. When I was alone, Starbucks would be an end-of-day reward for my busy day.

Michelle's first reaction to learning colors came as a shock. I pointed to the green logo on a Starbucks napkin during one of our morning visits and asked her what color it was. Her answer was "Starbucks."

I continued to do part-time consulting during this period until the marketing became too difficult to manage with three young kids. I accepted projects when they came along, but they gradually became few and far between. Eventually I took some time off to focus on the kids, although I honestly always felt caught between being a working mother and a stay-at-home mom. I had never enjoyed sitting still.

1998: Back to School

Michelle started preschool at the JCC in the fall of 1998 while simultaneously Bruce decided to go back to school for his MBA. Bruce took a leave of absence from June 1998 to June 1999 to study as part of the MIT Sloan Fellows Program. Instead of the experiencing the typical 40-year-old midlife crisis of buying a Jaguar convertible, Bruce decided to spend the year in an intense 12-month mid-career program for professionals who took a gap year from their jobs. The Sloan Fellows MBA is a prestigious program that accepts only fifty students annually. The class comprises future rising stars from large corporations worldwide. Past alumni have included Kofi Annan and Carly Fiorina.

Bruce's leave was unpaid, while everyone else in his class worked in private industry with full compensation and $80K tuition reimbursement, as well as living and entertainment expense accounts for their families. As mentioned, the class size was small, consisting of fifty Sloan Fellows.

Each class participant brought a partner, spouse and family, where applicable, to live in rented homes in the Cambridge and Metro-West area for the year. The Sloan Fellows came from all over the country and world. There were several families that rented homes close to us in Dover, Needham, and Wellesley. It was suggested that the spouses of the students form a "partners" program to support each other socially during the program year.

Over that summer our kids went to day camp at the JCC. I suggested meeting the nearby Sloan "partners" at the Needham Starbucks, since it was centrally located in MetroWest. We began to gather there after dropping the kids off at various day camps. As summer progressed, this became the "go to" meeting spot.

As the summer ended, we started a formal group and named it the "Sloan Fellows Partners Program." We organized get-togethers to plan activities for the visiting families. I again had the travel bug after meeting families from all over the world, and I embraced the opportunity to befriend as many classmates as possible. I was encouraged to join the board of directors because I was the "local" one. Whenever I travel, I always want to meet and learn from the locals, and thus I was elated to have evolved into the "local" for the Sloan class of 1999!

Over the course of the program, the Partners got to know each other and developed a few laughs and jokes. One woman's husband was named Joe, so the term "My Joe" became a popular phrase.

1999: Tour de France

In 1999 Starbucks introduced a series of coffee mugs and artwork by artist *M. Mark Slack Meyer* called **Tour de Java**. The main design image featured a French café in front of the Eiffel Tower. The Needham Starbucks had a prominent display of this image in a featured poster that I would often admire when meeting my friends for coffee.

In the final months of Bruce's MBA program, he was scheduled to take a two-week field trip to Europe. Since I hadn't traveled since the kids were born, my parents and in-laws agreed to watch them so I could join Bruce for part of his trip. I was able to join him during the Paris segment for a long weekend and receive a personal "Tour de Java." I shared this visit with Karen, my sister-in-law, and my almost sister-in-law Joyce (Karen's actual s-i-l) during a post-trip rendezvous at the Needham Starbucks.

Bruce graduated from the program in June 1999. To celebrate, Joyce gave us a numbered print of the Starbucks "Java" artwork as a graduation gift. I ended up buying the matching set of coffee mugs. We still have this framed piece in our kitchen.

Tour de Java

Fall 1999: Here Comes the Bus

Michelle started Kindergarten in the fall of 1999, and all three kids were now full-time students. I missed the busy-ness of having them home and craved a way to stay involved with their activities.

My consulting clients were dwindling, but I rapidly filled the time void. My first step was to become a "Room Mother" and eventually a PTO Board Member. My new vocation as a volunteer was launched and eventually evolved to Cub Scout Leader, Brownie and Girl Scout leader, Treasurer for PTO, room parent for each kid, Cheer Coach, and anything else that came across my option range. My friend Beth gave me a decorative towel that said, "When I say no, I feel guilty."

I became a professional expert in each group's mission and quickly learned how to manage multiple volunteer roles in a timely and efficient manner. Given my accounting background, the role of treasurer often became a natural fit for me. Each of these volunteer activities involved coordination and meetings with others.

Sometimes I ran back-to-back meetings at the Needham Starbucks, and everyone including the baristas knew my standard order: a Grande Dark Roast. My mom gave me a mug that said Starbucks was "my new office."

When I wasn't volunteering or running meetings, I frequently ran into friends during my visits to the Needham Starbucks. It was there that I learned about upcoming local events and children's activities. We would compare notes about the best extracurricular programs available for the kids, places to eat, weekend destinations, fun places to travel, shop, and much more. People began to recognize me as a regular and to ask me for "local" advice.

2000: It's a Small World After All (Although Not for Starbucks at the Time)

To celebrate New Year's Eve and the new millennium we went to Walt Disney World with about ten families from my high school graduation **Class of 1976** for a weeklong celebration. I was unable to find a Starbucks anywhere and was very disappointed. I learned that Nestlé had a huge stake in Walt Disney World and Disney could only carry their brand. I bought the available coffee, but it was much weaker and I felt withdrawal the entire week.

We had purchased yearlong Disney passes and went back the following December with our good friends, the Weinsteins, who also joined us the previous year. Again, I spent a week without Starbucks, but I compensated when I got back. At this point I wasn't too thrilled with Florida.

Disney 2000 Rachael, Greg bottom
Wendy Bruce middle and Michelle top

The following year my parents sold their Newton home and moved to Tarpon Springs, Florida, and my brother Max and I helped them settle in. They moved in early September 2002. I was very excited to see a Starbucks near their new condo at Eastlake, and this made me re-evaluate Florida. I patronized the local Starbucks whenever I visited my parents, and this helped reassure me that they were in a good place.

My parents, Herb and Audrey, Wendy and Maxwell

1999–2001: Life Is Not a Dress Rehearsal

My son Greg became interested in acting when he was in second grade. He launched his stage career as a magician and transitioned to stage performing after attending a summer arts camp at the JCC.

In fourth grade he was cast in his first major role in a community theater production of *Oliver* with the Dover Foundation. This coincided with Bruce's MBA year at Sloan. During this time, we lived in a raised ranch-style house and Bruce would spread out in the dining room to work on his thesis, expecting me to keep the three kids quiet.

Since it was almost impossible to keep the volume down, it became increasingly stressful at home. Starbucks became my refuge. With the girls in tow, we would drop Greg at rehearsal, go to Starbucks for a snack and come back to watch him rehearse.

We got to know many of the cast members at the community theater and truly enjoyed our time there. Greg had the role of the Junior Artful Dodger and a featured solo singing "Consider Yourself at Home." This became one of my favorite songs, and not just because I had become a Stage Mom. The wording became part of my MO as a hostess for years to come and I reflect on it whenever we have guests.

It was during this period that I developed my own love for the stage and aspired to become involved with the production. Although I had no theatrical aspirations myself, the show was an amazing experience for Greg.

The Dover Foundation theater group only performed limited shows with children on alternating years. For this particular show they brought in Keith Greenfield, a director who loved working with children.

After the show's final curtain, the twenty-plus children in the cast and their parents wanted more. I pushed Keith and helped organize the other parents to co-found a children's theater group in Dover called Open Fields. I soon became the Treasurer and producer. I continued to be a key Board member for the next ten-plus years.[13]

September 11

September 11 had been a special date since my early days of being introduced to drinking coffee as a youth. It was my Bat Mitzvah date in 1971. Thirty years later I was reminiscing about this day when a few hours later we heard news of the morning attacks on the World Trade Center.

I had just left Starbucks to attend a PTO meeting in Dover. As I entered the meeting room, one member had just learned of the attack on the first tower. We were each rattled, and our meeting was quickly upended. During the days that followed we were all in shock, just like the rest of the world.

The evening of September 11, 2001, was supposed to be the initial rehearsal to launch Open Fields's first mainstage show, *The Wizard of Oz*. At Keith's suggestion, I had agreed to be a co-producer for this show although I had zero experience. We decided to cancel rehearsal that night and postpone the scheduled read-through. We did have rehearsal a few days later to maintain a semblance of normalcy for the kids. After reminiscing about the peace and solace I had found at rehearsals of *Oliver* a few years earlier, this was a welcome decision.

Participating in this production helped launch my involvement in community theater. All three kids were cast in the show: Greg played a junior version of the Lion, and Rachael and Michelle were cast as Munchkins. After September 11 I spent much of my time at rehearsals and then offsite working my producer role, often at the Needham Starbucks. This certainly was on-the-job training and became a full-time effort for about three months. I never came to rehearsal without bringing a takeout cup of Starbucks, and soon everyone recognized my devotion to coffee.

2001: *I Wanna Be a Producer*

    I have been involved with community theater since the inception of Open Fields in 2000. All three kids continued to be active in this group as well as in middle and high school shows. This became a family endeavor, as Bruce often helped with set building during these productions. I produced over thirty shows during these years and am still involved in local community theater, both for the Dover Foundation and my synagogue, Temple Aliyah in Needham. In addition, I served as president for three years in addition to a prior role as treasurer on the board of Friends of Performing Arts (FOPA) while Greg was in high school. My FOPA involvement continued for a span of close to ten years until Michelle graduated. After Michelle's graduation I joined the Dover Foundation Board and have since chaired the Dover Cultural Council (a Town of Dover Government appointment) for almost nine years.

During rehearsals for school and community theater plays when I was often the producer, it became known that I would do coffee runs and volunteer to bring a "Box of Joe" to set-building days.

2002: To Life, to Life, to Starbucks

There was a pharmacy a few doors down from the Needham Starbucks that had great slush (a fruit-flavored frozen drink) for a dollar. Often the kids wanted a slush as a snack before Hebrew School or on a warm summer day after camp. Sometimes I would run into my sister-in-law Karen and my nieces Samantha and Jessie at Starbucks, and we would let the kids go to the pharmacy to get a slush while we chatted.

After performing in *The Wizard of Oz*, Greg wanted to continue pursuing community theater and soon auditioned and was cast in an ensemble role for Needham Community Theater's production of *Fiddler on the Roof*. The theater bug had become part of him.

The girls also caught the bug and followed Greg to Charles River Creative Arts Camp (CRCAP) for several summers. Coincidentally, my nieces (as mentioned above), as well as my niece Shira (Max's daughter), and extended family (Joyce's kids) also ended up at CRCAP for a few overlapping summers. Of course, all good days started with a Starbucks run after carpool drop-off.

When we planned Greg's Bar Mitzvah in 2002, I asked for permission to serve Starbucks coffee during the reception as the Temple coffee was pretty bad. My request was approved as "kosher," and slowly but surely the religious school teachers started asking me to bring them a cup if I was headed there during Hebrew lessons.

One night when the kids were a bit older, the Needham Starbucks had a karaoke Friday night. We went with my sister and brother-in-law (Karen and Donald) and our five combined kids. We were laughing at one of the baristas who sang the chicken dance song. Chicken is a traditional food to eat on Friday evening Shabbat dinners, so maybe it was good timing. To this day we still joke about that memorable evening.

Part Three:
Nest Starting to Empty

2005–2008:
Becoming a Local One

As the kids grew up, they became interested in many extracurricular activities beyond theater. Because Dover is a small town, most of these endeavors took place in surrounding communities where they became involved in cheerleading, ice hockey, gymnastics, sewing, magic lessons for Greg, and other performance art type programs. I had opportunities to meet and connect with other parents and community members involved in these pursuits. This helped expand my knowledge base of Metro-west and beyond. I am an explorer and one who always wants to see what is going on around me. As such, my reputation as a community resource became widely known among my Dover peers.

We had started to search for a larger home before Bruce began his MBA program, but our hunt went on hiatus as we partially funded Sloan tuition with our down-payment money. We were not able to resume our search until about five years later when Greg was a junior in high school.

This time, we did find a house we really liked, and we moved in 2005. During the process of buying our new home and listing our old one I became intrigued with the idea of becoming a Realtor. Since most of the in-town real estate agents knew me and were aware of my involvement in the community, they would often refer to me as the "local" expert on theater and other kids' activities. When someone Jewish moved to town, in particular, they would ask me about local synagogues and Jewish community resources. I was often sharing my knowledge to help them make a sale. Bruce suggested I become a Realtor and make money instead of helping everyone else succeed. Somewhat intrigued after our search, I began to explore this idea.

2007: Reality Launches My Realty

Greg left home to attend New York University in the fall of 2007. I felt a huge void when he went away and needed something to keep my mind focused. In addition, we would soon need to pay overlapping college tuition bills for all three kids. Thus, this became the right time to take the real estate licensing course. I took the class during that fall and passed the exam on my first try. I have since been a licensed Realtor.

After getting my license I was excited to meet friends to share the launch of my new profession. I initially joined Carlson GMAC in South Natick. After I had been there for a short time, Carlson was sold off and then dissolved. At that point in early 2008, I joined Hammond Residential Real Estate in Wellesley Center. Hammond was under the same umbrella as Carlson had been before they dissolved, and many of my colleagues moved there as well.

A major draw to Hammond was the office's proximity to the Wellesley Starbucks. Wellesley had their original store in the center of town, located in a converted Coffee Connection with proximity to Wellesley College. In addition, they opened a second store on Linden Street in a residential shopping plaza. Networking is encouraged to meet and share information within your sphere of influence, and of course I started meeting friends at Starbucks to talk about life and real estate. I would rotate between the two locations, often going to the center store during work hours and the Linden Street when socializing. One such visit became a life-changing event.

2008: Delilah

One day in mid-July 2008 I was scheduled to meet with my friend Rob Brandt at the Starbucks on Linden Street in Wellesley. Rob texted me that he was going to be late, so I sat and read the *Boston Globe*. Our family had talked about getting a Havanese dog for a few years, and I was skimming the pet section of the classified ads when I saw a breeder advertising a new litter of Havanese puppies. Excitedly, I made an appointment to visit his kennel in Concord that night. We met, fell in love, and adopted our dog Delilah. If Rob hadn't been late that day for our meeting at Starbucks, would I have discovered her? I often ask myself this question and thank Starbucks for making this coffee connection. It was one of my best.

Delilah has a strong innate sense of smell and she will tug on her leash whenever we walk by a Starbucks. She will stop in her tracks in front of the Mashpee Commons shop. She always welcomes water in a plastic Starbucks take-out cup. I also use the grande size cup to measure her dog food. She is a Starbucks pup. Like my youngest daughter Michelle, she has been indoctrinated to Starbucks since a very young age and recognizes the familiar logo.

Delilah at Starbucks

It's Too Early to Get Up, or Time for a Night Cap

Both of my daughters were cheerleaders and played ice hockey through middle and high school. Cheer practice started in late summer and continued until late fall. We met on hot summer eves and continued into cold wintry ones under Friday night lights as the season progressed. Varsity Ice Hockey practice took place early in the morning, often 5:30 a.m., at a rink about 40 minutes from home. The girls had to be fully uniformed and on the ice by the time practice began. This meant leaving the house before the crack of dawn on bone-chilling mornings. Ugh…. The only salvation was dropping them off and doing a coffee run while they were on the ice or later in the day before cheer practice. For ice hockey I would head to a nearby Starbucks that opened at 6:00 a.m. and often be first in line at the drive-up window. During cheer practice I would get a hot drink to keep me warm while sitting in the bleachers or walking around the field with a few moms.

After football season ended, the girls did competitive cheerleading and participated in tournaments throughout New England as well as a few out-of-state competitions including Rhode Island, Florida, Arizona, and Las Vegas. Except for the tournaments at the Dunkin' Convention Center in Providence, Starbucks was always the destination of choice.

2009–2012:
European Café Culture

A year after Greg had left for college, I still felt a deep void in my life. During Greg's freshman year I got my Real Estate license, and then soon after we got Delilah. I experienced the empty nest syndrome feeling whenever I walked by our son's neat but quiet bedroom. By Greg's sophomore year we had decided to explore the possibility of hosting an American Field Service (AFS) Student.

First, Naomi

We hosted two AFS foreign exchange students over the course of Rachael and Michelle's high school years. Naomi, our first, was from Vienna, Austria. She lived with us for six months in the winter and spring of 2009 during Rachael's junior year in high school. Naomi arrived bringing a famous

Austrian cake called a Sacher-torte, and she shared how she often went to the Viennese cafés. I quickly assumed she was a huge coffee drinker, and as her introduction to the Boston area I took her on daily tours of local Starbucks coffee shops. She had extreme jetlag initially and craved the caffeine. Spending time together at Starbucks became a regular venture.

Our daughter Rachael visited Naomi in Austria the following summer when she was 16, and Naomi took her to all the cafés in Vienna. The difference, however, is that the cafés Naomi frequented served alcohol, which was legal for minors in Europe.

Left to right, Naomi, Rachael, Michelle, and Wendy

Next, Our Italian Son

In Fall 2010, Rachael was off to study at Dartmouth College, and our house became even emptier. During the summer of 2011 when Michelle was a rising high school junior, we decided to host another AFS foreign exchange student. This time we thought it would be fun to have a male, so we invited Samuele from Italy to be our son for the coming year. Our family had always loved Italian food and had been interested in Italian culture. Samuele lived with us for a full year. He became an amazing cook over his year with us and introduced our family to many new recipe ideas.

I shared my love of coffee with Samuele. He actually was a coffee lover. We would often go out for visits to local Starbucks throughout the year. He has been back to visit us a few times, and we typically start each visit with a Starbucks stop. We visited his family in Monselice, Italy, in 2016. Samuele's mom makes the true Italian espresso brew at their home every morning.

Left to right, Michelle, Rachael, Wendy, and Samuele

In the spring before Samuele's arrival, as I walked into the Needham Starbucks, I noticed that a new Driver's Ed school was opening next door. I went in to meet the instructors and learn about their offerings. The day Michelle was eligible for Driver's Ed I signed her up. As they often say in real estate, "location, location, location." Thus, the ulterior motive for selecting this location was clearly the ability to drop her off and wait at Starbucks.

Michelle got her driver's license at the end of junior year and could soon drive to school. This allowed me to sleep in a bit later in the morning. During Michelle's first six months of driving, she could only transport siblings. Since Samuele was on the same school schedule as Michelle, we made it officially known that he was our Italian son. I was totally free from carpooling responsibilities.

Wendy, Greg, Michelle, Samuele, Rachael, and Bruce

Don't Leave Home Without It

In 2001, Starbucks introduced a prepaid card to use for coffee purchases. This became a standard birthday gift for me to give others, although I was always thrilled to be on the receiving end.[14]

Around 2010 Starbucks added the concept of Starbucks online accounts and eventually the Starbucks App. Like

American Express, Starbucks membership has its privileges, and members are encouraged to register gift cards online to track and begin to earn points towards free drinks. Within a year of opening my account I achieved Gold Level status, which is based on annual purchase volume. After about 18 months and ever since 2011 I have always maintained Gold Level for up to two years in the future. I guess I drink too much coffee, and this prompted my husband to invest in Starbucks stock.

To this day I have always maintained a balance on my Starbucks account. My philosophy is that I always want to be able to grab a coffee even if I forget my wallet.

Camp Bornstein and the Summer of 2008

Before our exchange students lived with us, we invited our niece Shira to stay with us during the summer months and called our house ***Camp Bornstein***. She attended Charles River day camp and other area programs with the kids through high school. I would pick them up at camp (CRCAP) in my Ford Expedition (named BIGRED for the carpool lane) and we would often head to our usual Needham venue. Shira became a regular slush and Starbucks junkie with my kids for years to come.

Big Red

When Shira was a rising high school sophomore during the summer of 2008, she attended a program at Wellesley College called Explorations. She stayed at our house and I drove her to and from campus every day for about four weeks. The upside of this was the opportunity to increase my Starbucks points with frequent visits. During the same summer, Rachael and Michelle attended a sewing camp and had pre-season cheerleading practice. Shira and I spent many an evening grabbing a brew and watching them from the sidelines.

One afternoon I went to pick Shira up at her program, knowing she was going to explore Wellesley Center and the Starbucks nearby with her Explorations group. I spotted the campers and said hello to her before the Camp Counselor stated that she wasn't allowed to talk to anyone outside the group. I guess I looked like a scary suburban mom drinking coffee. After meeting up at the appropriate pickup spot at day end, we headed off for our nightly Cheer rounds. I learned to respect Explorations protocols.

Running on Starbucks, not Dunkin...

The halfway point of the Boston Marathon is Wellesley Center. Almost perfectly centered on the Mile 13 mark is the Starbucks. Every year I would take the kids to watch the marathon when they were young, and after they moved on, I brought Delilah to watch from my Starbucks vantage point with my coffee in hand.

Boston Marathon, Mile 13

On another note, every year the town of Wellesley hosts a Thanksgiving morning Turkey Trot. The starting point is the Linden Street Starbucks. For those who haven't spent time in New England, Thanksgiving morning can be quite cold and there is nothing like a hot cup of coffee after running a 5K when the outside temperature is under 10 degrees. After completing the 5K, my daughter Michelle and I looked forward to this reward for our efforts.

Turkey Trot with Michelle

When in Rome, Do Like the Romans

Whenever I travel, I tell my family I want to meet the locals. I always try to research local websites and buy tour books that highlight local neighborhoods and places off the beaten path. My kids always laugh when I say I want to meet "the locals."

I read former Starbucks CEO Howard Schultz's book, *Pour Your Heart Into It: How Starbucks Built a Company One Cup at a Time*,[15] when it first came out in the late 1990s. His inspiration for Starbucks dates back to a vacation in Italy. He was drawn to romanticism and the fresh aroma of coffee during his visit. He knew that cafés were a big part of European culture, and he had the vision to bring this experience to the States.

Schultz imagined having cafés with a high standard brand that could become a destination for every American. He was an early visionary on the start of coffee culture in the

States. One of his key philosophies was to stick to the basic mission of coffee and not serve foods that would take away from the caffeine aroma. His vision was to stay true to the mission of bringing high-quality coffee to every street corner in America. He also envisioned having each shop fit in with the local architecture.

After reading Schultz's book I developed a preconceived image of Italians sitting around sipping coffee at the local cafés, but I quickly learned that this was an American thing. When we visited Italy in 2016, in fact, I was almost chased out of a café in Venice by an angry barista who said, "no loitering." The Italians buy their espresso shots and sip them down quickly, almost like an energy boost. I never got used to the espressos and stuck with Café Americanos in Italy.

Left to right, Greg, Michelle, Bruce, Wendy, and Rachael

Beyond Rome

Whenever I travel, I am quick to notice whether there is a Starbucks nearby. Even seeing a Starbucks upon landing at the airport when approaching a new destination makes me feel welcome in an unfamiliar place. I equate this with the feeling I get from seeing the Statue of Liberty when visiting New York. Maybe it is my initial coffee snobbishness, but I think having a local Starbucks says good things about a community.

I have often touted the idea of having a Starbucks passport that I could get stamped for each new one I visit. I think this may have been created.

Many places adapt their local Starbucks to blend in with the community vibe. There is an awesome one in Prague at the top of the great wall up near the Palace. Maui has a beautiful one near Ka'ana'pali surrounded by palm trees.

In the UK the Starbucks was very similar to the ones in the States. I even thought the pricing was the same after seeing my usual grande for £1.65. Little did I realize until I got my credit card statement that at the time the Euro exchange was 2:1 to the US dollar and my coffee habit was a bit pricey.

Although some may say Starbucks is a sign of The Greening of America,[16] I always check it out as a first stop. However, depending on where I am, I will then be open to trying some local brews as well.

2007-2013: *In Sickness and in Health*

Around the time of Michelle's Bat Mitzvah, my dad started to have some serious health issues. I went to visit him in the hospital in downtown Tampa, Florida, where he had aspirating pneumonia. Both my parents made a point of telling me that I would like the hospital because it had a Starbucks in it. Although I had never liked hospitals, this was the only saving grace. I have since had to spend much time in hospitals and rehabilitation facilities as my parents' health declined. I would go to Starbucks to take a break and recharge so I would be able to deal with the situation at hand. Starbucks would be my place of solace and trust throughout the good and the bad times.

My dad passed away in 2013 in Florida. In the months before his death, I would visit him often and he would continue to share his words of wisdom, expecting me to hold a coffee in hand. He would always joke that I should get an "IV" connected to a Starbucks coffee urn while he was connected to one for his nutrition.

A year after Dad passed, my mom was diagnosed with pancreatic cancer. She came to live with us in Dover during the course of her treatment. Mom's mainstay every morning was a cup of coffee, although I got her to graduate from Maxwell House to Starbucks. She still made coffee first thing every morning to drink while reading the print newspaper.

At home in Massachusetts, my first cup of the day was always at a Starbucks. When I was at my mom's home in Florida, she would prepare the coffee maker the night before with a pre-set timer to be ready when she awoke. I became her coffee timer at our house, and she wanted me to join her for a cup every morning. We would chat and start our day together this way for close to six months. When she finished her treatment, Mom was able to return to Florida where she later passed away in July 2015. My brother and I were with her during the final days. To this day I brew a pot of coffee first thing every morning, read the paper, and think of her.

A little while before my dad passed away, my in-laws moved into an assisted living facility near their home of fifty years in Needham. They were not coffee drinkers, and before they moved from their primary home they would always offer me a cup of Nescafé instant coffee whenever I visited. Since I was not an instant coffee drinker, it became a ritual to stop at Starbucks before each visit. My father-in-law Joe would joke that one time when he came to my house, I made him a cup of coffee that kept him awake for days. When I brought coffee when visiting him, he would always say "Wendy and her cup of Joe." Another "Joe" was in my life.

2008–2013: A Cup of Coffee and a Good Book

There is nothing as rewarding as reading a good book while enjoying a cup of coffee, although I often find it difficult to find the time to read as much as I would like.

I thought it was a brilliant idea when Barnes & Nobles introduced their in-store cafés and even better when they allowed Starbucks to run it. I was raised in a home of avid readers.

My mom loved her morning cup paired with reading the daily newspaper. She always enjoyed a good novel, too. My dad loved history, and over his lifetime he amassed a library of over 10,000 books. He was always on the hunt for another addition to the collection. During my visits when he was healthy, he could spend hours at the Barnes & Noble near his Florida home, and you can guess where I would be waiting for him.

I inherited my love of books from my dad and my love of coffee from my mom. The combination of the two was a match made in heaven. I read a broad range of books, including historical fiction, novels, and some nonfiction. Before spending hours looking at the "staff recommendations" at Barnes & Noble, I would grab a cup of coffee and then schmooze. I would never leave empty-handed. I often read eBooks on my Kindle now but still enjoy the opportunity to visit a brick-and-mortar bookstore.

Likewise, I often see people reading at Starbucks. I will strike up a conversation when I see someone in line holding a book to ask them how they like it. I am never too shy to ask someone what book they are reading.

As mentioned, finding time to read can be challenging. At home I often find myself sidetracked with projects to tackle or phone calls to make. To make time for reading in recent years, I have used my calendar to make reading appointments for myself at the local Starbucks. I enjoy pairing a visit with a reading session, sometimes sitting in a comfortable chair incognito where no one will bother me. I will put my phone on silent mode and grab a coffee, sit back, and delve into the book with minimal distractions. I will set a reading goal, as I always need to finish the chapter before I leave. If the book is really good, I may be tempted to continue reading and go on to the next chapter.

82

Since I am often reading at Starbucks, I came up with the idea of hosting a book signing to help my friend Michael King launch his book *Patriots Passion from Day One* when he published it in 2012. I helped Michael with marketing on a pro bono basis and served as his public relations person. In fact, Michael was a major inspiration to me when I decided to write this book.

Michael King signing at Starbucks in Needham

I set up a book signing for Michael at a table in the Needham Starbucks on a weekday morning. It was fun, and we sold a few copies. This venture also resulted in a new coffee connection which continues to this day.

A woman I met at Starbucks, Mimi Segel, suggested that I connect with a colleague of hers, Kevin Walsh, who worked as a sportscaster at Comcast SportsNet New England and NECN. In addition to his sportscasting job, he had just published his first book, titled *The Marrow in Me,* and was eager to start marketing it locally. Mimi suggested that I reach out to Kevin, since she saw how I was helping Michael. I always follow through with potential connections and happily reached out to Kevin.

I met Kevin at the Wellesley Starbucks to learn about his book. He and I clicked and have since become good friends. As a result of this connection I had him help champion a bone marrow drive at Dover Sherborn High School for a teacher who was critically ill and needed a match. The school hosted a program called "Meet the Match," and Kevin helped by attending the drive and sharing insight into his personal experience of becoming a bone marrow donor, which he chronicled in his book. He has since written a few other books and always contacts me pre-publication. In addition, last year he launched a podcast called "Why I Read Non-Fiction." I was his seventh guest on June 3, 2019.[17] This is a friendship that started through a Starbucks connection and even led to me finding the publisher for this book.

Part Four:
Empty Nest Syndrome

KARMA

This is not the end of your story; it is merely the beginning of a new chapter.

2013: First Symptom: a Mac Attack

My knowledge of both the local market and community are the tools I use every day to build and promote my real estate business. Upon reflection, I now realize I have become the "local one" that I had wanted to meet many years ago.

Michelle headed to Tufts University in the fall of 2013. After all three kids got Macintosh computers when starting college, I decided it was time for me to upgrade my business tools. I always saw business professionals sitting at Starbucks with their laptops in tow and had laptop envy. I wanted to follow this trend. My first laptop was a 20" Macbook Pro because Bruce thought I needed a big screen. It was a bit too heavy and hurt my shoulder to carry around.

It wasn't until I bought my 13" Macbook Air that I started to spend time working predominantly at Starbucks rather than the office. When I was at Hammond Residential Real Estate in Wellesley, the founder and president Saul Cohen always told us we should never be *"Secret Agents."* He said we should figure out how to tell everyone what we do and when in public, share what we do even if subliminally. Little things like sitting with a laptop to work at the coffee shop and wearing a nametag would be ways for others to see that we were Realtors. I took this advice to heart, especially after acquiring my Mac. I moved to Coldwell Banker in Needham in 2015 and have since made the Needham Starbucks my official offsite office.

Until Michelle graduated from high school in 2013, I would primarily visit the Needham or Wellesley Starbucks. While coaching high school cheerleading for Michelle's team, I would often run to one of these Starbucks before practice. The fall after she graduated, a new Starbucks opened in Medfield, which is much closer to the high school. This would become the venue for my non-work-related meetings. I was already involved in community theater, and as mentioned previously, soon became chairperson of the Dover Cultural Council and joined the board of directors for the Dover Foundation.

In addition, in 2014 I became the producer of *Fiddler on the Roof* for my Temple's Fiftieth Anniversary production. This coincided with the time when my mom was ill and stayed with us. While she napped, I would often have meetings at Starbucks to give her some quiet time. I was often asked whether I wanted to pull away from producing when I became her primary care provider, but again, I found solace in the combination of musical theater and the relaxation time I could spend at Starbucks.

A year after *Fiddler,* I coerced the production team from the show (director, stage manager, and choreographer) to team up with me again when I was selected to be producer of *The Pirates of Penzance* in 2016 for the Dover Foundation. Another member of the group, Ruth, agreed to serve as assistant producer and help with publicity. She was an avid Starbucks drinker like me, and the Medfield Starbucks became our weekly meeting spot. Since we all loved good coffee, we ended up serving Starbucks during intermissions. I believe a good cup of coffee is the key to staying awake and enjoying the show!

To this day, I am actively involved in all aspects of the performing arts and often hold meetings at a nearby Starbucks. I also promote serving Starbucks coffee during intermission at the concession stand.

There's an App for That

I can't remember exactly when I downloaded the Starbucks App, but I think it was during the 2016 production of *Pirates.* Lisa, our stage manager, was also an ardent Starbucks coffee drinker. She was one up on me and actually introduced me to the Starbucks App. Until I met Lisa, I had thought I was the coffee expert. The App became a game changer.

I could now order a cup on the App and then quickly run in to grab my coffee when I was on my way somewhere. Besides the perks of earning stars, the App makes ordering much easier. And when the line is particularly long, I can avoid the wait by ordering ahead of time.

Another huge plus is that I can use the App to order a cup during a walk with Delilah. When I arrive at Starbucks, my coffee is ready for me to run in and grab. When I'm en route to work, I can order a cup while I'm waiting for a traffic light to turn green and time it so my coffee is available for pick-up when I get there. It is sometimes a close call to be on time for work, but I always take the risk.

If I am on vacation or not in a rush to be somewhere, I often enjoy waiting in line and chatting with the other patrons. This gives me a chance to feel the vibe and meet the "locals."

Starbucks always has promotions to motivate customers to earn stars based on making a certain number of purchases within a specific time span. Shhh… I don't want to widely publicize this, but if I need to place five orders to achieve a status, sometimes I will order individually for family members instead of doing a bulk order.

I am a cheap date and a simple grande dark roast girl. I don't go for the fancy brews or sweet drinks. I am always happy with my basic brewed coffee. This is a 50-star drink that I would rarely use points for unless I am totally out of cash. I prefer to accumulate my points and at times have had over 1000, although my total usage has been lower during the pandemic and some of my points have expired.

When I do use my reward points, it is to treat my family to the higher-end, expensive drinks. It kills me to pay five-plus dollars for a beverage. When I do splurge, it is for a "Matcha Iced Tea Latte" or sometimes a dry cappuccino.

Sometimes You Just Need to Sneak in a Cup

I now have an empty nest. There are long hours of work for Bruce, and sometimes my real estate business is slow. I will share how I spent my free time as an empty nester, first pre-COVID and then later under the new "normal."

My daily routine would be to go to the JCC for a yoga or Pilates class and afterwards stop at Starbucks, Trader Joe's, and CVS or take care of local errands on the way home. Using Starbucks for a few minutes of Zen, I would plan out the rest of my other daily tasks.

When I had more time to spend at Starbucks, I would also indulge my love of reading. To appear highly visible (not a **Secret Agent**) if I was not busy with real estate work I would periodically set up my laptop to check emails and social media before reading my Kindle.

I enjoy reading self-improvement or personal development books and treat these like a mini self-help course for my soul. If I wasn't working on client tasks, I sometimes dedicated quality time to reading these books during my Starbucks mornings. Two inspiring books most recently read were *Midlife: A Philosophical Guide*[18] and *Crucial Conversations*.[19] I would then look forward to incorporating the lessons learned from each book into my persona.

As I read *Midlife*, for example, I started to think more about my personal relationships and how I view the approach I often take to things I do. Principle terms introduced in the book are "Telic" and "Atelic." To describe these briefly, one who is "atelic" enjoys the journey to a destination, while someone who is "telic" focuses on getting to the destination.

Crucial Conversations gave me insight into how to handle conversations, especially when confronting someone whom I perceived as an adversary. A key point brought out was that most people are insecure and often build a wall of defense around them to protect against perceived threats. We sometimes avoid speaking to others because we feel insecure that they will attack this barrier. It is important to frame a conversation in a manner that is non-threatening and allows the other person to feel welcome to share their perspective. I soon took what I learned from this book to a new level.

Bruce and I spent a weekend at Mohegan Sun (a casino-resort in Connecticut) during the same week that Attorney General Jeff Sessions had announced that illegal immigrants would be separated from their children at the border and put in cages. I was understandably upset about this latest news cycle story and was standing in line behind an older man who was wearing a bright red MAGA hat.

Since the line moved slowly and my spot lasted for more than 10 minutes, I asked the man in front of me if he really thought the president was making America great again. I decided this was an opportunity to learn what someone wearing a MAGA hat thought, since most people I associate with at my usual Starbucks shared viewpoints similar to mine. He told me how upset he was that his daughter who lived in a southern state was not able to get some type of insurance coverage and he thought the government was giving it away to "illegals." I shared my concern about separating children from their parents and asked how that would improve his daughter's circumstances. He could not answer my question. I then shared that his daughter should research Medicaid programs in her state, and I mentioned that putting children in cages would not help his daughter. He was thankful for my suggestion.

I then told him I had just read a great book and mentioned the key skills of learning how to better understand the viewpoints of others in order to converse without becoming confrontational. I commented that this was an important skill that all Americans could use to overcome being so divided. He saw me drinking my coffee a bit later and approached to greet and ask me for the name of the book I had mentioned earlier. This was indeed a "Crucial Conversation."

Another beloved pastime of mine is going to movie theaters. Last winter I purchased an AMC movie pass and found myself seeing at least one movie per week. During Oscar season, I met my annual challenge of seeing all of the nominated films before awards night.

My favorite day starts with a pre-movie visit to Starbucks and continues by sipping my takeout brew during the show. I find that whenever I get a chance to sit still, I have been known to doze off. Just the aroma and psychology of having a cup in hand helps me stay awake. Even if I don't drink the coffee, my brain stays more awake.

While some theaters have started to feature "Starbucks brewed here," I have found that movie theater coffee is often old and stale tasting; thus, I prefer to bring my own. Because many theaters sell their own overpriced, over-brewed coffee, they do not allow outside drinks.

There have been many times when I have had to sneak coffee in. After a few tries I have learned the best approach and can usually slip it by the ticket collector, although I have been stopped once or twice. This is particularly irritating when you have a new cup and can't finish it before the movie starts.

At an AMC in Union Square NYC I was almost chased out of the theater and refused admission until I finished my drink. The ticket taker threatened to call the NYPD if my daughter Michelle and I didn't discard our coffees. I thought, "Really, don't they have better things to focus on?"

In addition, there is a ticket taker at AMC in Framingham who caught on to my efforts and started following me whenever I showed him my admission tickets. I soon learned how to hide a cup under my left arm inside my jacket. This is difficult in the warmer months and can raise suspicion when bringing a sweatshirt on a 90-degree day. I have had a few spills. I must admit that AMC staff are extremely dedicated and loyal employees.

When I produce a show, I always try to serve Starbucks at the concession table both pre-show and during intermission, as I know firsthand how much this is appreciated. Although we don't allow food in the theater, if the cup has a lid we will allow patrons to "sneak" it in.

On a weekly basis I have looked forward to meeting my sister-in-law Karen and local friends to catch up on the events in our lives. Karen would often join me at the movies. Sometimes I set daily goals and then reward myself by meeting friends for coffee at the end of a busy day. A quick Starbucks meetup is always a fun way to top off the day.

On the Road Again

Delilah, my travel companion.

I travel a lot more now that the kids are out of the house. My kids have moved to New Hampshire, New York, Ann Arbor, San Francisco, and most recently Miami. Occasionally Bruce travels for work. I would take advantage of any opportunity available to visit the kids, join Bruce on business trips, and turn any and all of these into mini-vacations. I also enjoy visiting my brother's family in Baltimore when possible. I love to travel and see new places.

For domestic travel, particularly for road trips, I study the map to figure out which rest stops along the highways have a Starbucks.

Whether I am traveling domestically or internationally, I always use my Starbucks App to see where the closest café will be to my destination. I typically visit this venue the first day of my itinerary. As I venture out and explore a bit further, however, I am a strong believer in checking out the local coffee scene.

For example, when I'm in Brooklyn or the Lower East Side I will scout out local cafés. A good sign is if you see a barista and freshly ground coffee. A good aroma is a positive sign. I will admit I visited **Gregory's Coffee** primarily because I liked the name (and their coffee was quite tasty).

In San Francisco there are a number of great places, such as the **Verve**. This place is so popular that it is a featured café at the company where my daughter Rachael works. Her company also has their own baristas and cafés throughout their business campus. They operate free full-service cafés as a perk to employees, and we went to a few of them during my last visit. Today's business climate is different from the corporate experience I had in the 1980s.

Whenever I head toward New York or go west on the Mass Pike, my first stop is always the Starbucks at the intersection of Route 27 and Route 30. This is known to be one of the busiest in the state. In Connecticut there is a nice one in Westport near Route 1 that I try to hold out for on my way to NYC. Likewise, when heading further south toward Delaware, I stop along the Jersey turnpike, typically at the Thomas Edison or Woodrow Wilson Plaza, and then stop again on Route 95 upon entering Maryland.

Our family was in NYC in January 2020 for the wedding of the daughter of our family friends, the Weinsteins. After the event we spent a freezing-cold afternoon walking Hudson Yard on the West Side. We all craved a warm drink and ventured to check out the new **Starbucks Reserve**. It was one of the first Reserves and was located near the Chelsea Market. We were chilled to the bone, and this was a perfect spot to warm up. The place is like a museum and fun to visit, although personally I am a simplistic dark roast coffee drinker and found it a bit pricey for my wallet. We spent a good hour defrosting with our reserve blends.

The following month we visited San Francisco to see Michelle and Rachael, as Michelle had just moved out west. We stayed with Rachael and her boyfriend, Aaron, and toured Danville, California, to spend the day with Michelle and her boyfriend, Alex and his family. We again had the opportunity to visit the newest **Reserve** in this bedroom community. It had a really nice venue and was a great place to sit, chat, and have a family photo opp. The coffee was amazing, too.

Starbucks Reserve in Danville

The next month the pandemic hit, and there have been no more travels for a long time. I'm looking forward to the next time I can safely be on the road again.

Other Good Brews Along My Travels

In Israel, we discovered **Aroma,** which has amazing coffee and makes one of the best cappuccinos I ever had.

Our visit to Aroma stands out for more than the coffee experience. Bruce, Michelle, and I were in Israel in 2016 for my nephew Eric's Bar Mitzvah in 2016 and had a celebratory dinner with family at the Port of Tel Aviv. We went for a long walk toward the port area during the day, and then it started to rain. There was a random shooting nearby in Tel Aviv. We stopped in Aroma just to dry off and have a break. Suddenly the streets were on lockdown. We ended up spending close to three hours in Aroma and sampled a bunch of their food options as well as coffee offerings. This was one of the few times that we spent a sizeable stint together at a coffee shop.

Bruce at Aroma in Tel Aviv

My Favorite Hot Spots

I am a regular at a few Starbucks, but the Highland Avenue location in Needham has been my mainstay. This was the one where I raised my kids and went whenever I was on a carpool shift for Hebrew School. When my son attended Prozdor (a religious high school program) in Newton, I would drive him on Sunday mornings and hang out at the Starbucks that used to be on Union Street. That shop has been relocated near the corner of Center and Beacon Street.

When I worked in the Hammond office in Wellesley, I would go to the Wellesley Center Starbucks before my call shift or during breaks. When not working, I would frequent the Linden Street one, as it has a nice outdoor area and I could go there with Delilah. In fact, as previously mentioned, this is the one where I found the advertisement for a Havanese puppy, so I consider it a special place for both of us. Perhaps that's why I use a Starbucks cup to scoop out her food. Post-COVID, this has become my go-to place because they have an outdoor seating area and ample socially distanced seating.

When Greg was in middle school, our family attended the Society of Young Magicians (SYM) Conference held in April at the Seacrest Motel in Falmouth on Cape Cod. During his sessions, the rest of us had free time and explored the Falmouth area. We soon discovered the drive-through Starbucks in Falmouth on Route 28. This became part of our daily morning routine for the duration of the three-day conference.

During school rehearsals and sports practice at the high school it was a close call distance-wise between the Starbucks in Westwood and Wellesley. I would go to Westwood once in a while but found the service a bit too laid back.

Once all three kids were out of school, in the fall of 2013 Starbucks opened in Medfield on the border of Main and Route 109. I now go there when I have to head toward Medfield for errands. I wish this Starbucks had opened when my kids were in high school, particularly during all their rehearsals and sporting events. It has a nice outdoor café, and as mentioned elsewhere is a convenient place to meet for Dover-related business.

When we venture to spend a day in Boston, we love the Starbucks on the corner of Beacon and Arlington Street. Sometimes we have gone to events at the Boston Commons, and this is always a great first stop.

Family at Boston Public Garden with Samuele

During the summers before we bought our Cape beach house, we used to stay at the Radisson Inn in Hyannis. There was no Starbucks in the Hyannis area, but the Barnes & Noble at the Hyannis Mall sold "Starbucks-brewed" coffee. It was the next best thing, as Hyannis had no good local coffee shops.

Eventually we discovered Mashpee Commons around 2010 and started to take day trips to the area, which had an outside shopping mall. We grew to love the area, and in 2015 bought a townhouse nearby. The Mashpee Starbucks has since become my favorite go-to place in the summer. Pre-pandemic, I went there almost every day to walk Delilah and get a morning brew. Delilah recognizes this location and will pull me toward it whenever we are nearby.

Delilah at Mashpee Commons

One of my favorite memories of this shop is something that happened last summer. I was getting coffee with my friend Jayne when suddenly tornado alerts hit our phones. All patrons were told to evacuate because the windows could shatter. It was unsafe to drive, and the manager from L.L. Bean across the street invited all of us to wait out the storm in their safer brick-walled store. We sipped our coffee in the shoe department through the storm's duration. To this day Jayne and I share this memory and laugh about it, especially when meeting for coffee.

Riding out the storm at L.L. Bean

Although I don't frequent these coffee shops often, when I do spend time on the Cape I enjoy an occasional random visit to **Cape Cod Coffee** in Mashpee, **Coffee Obsession** in Falmouth and Woods Hole, as well as **The Wired Puppy** in Provincetown. While Cape Cod Coffee offers excellent home-cooked food to accompany their local brew, the latter two have been known to reflect my frequently noted coffee state of mind.

Wired Puppy in Provincetown

I also really like the Waban Starbucks and will go there whenever I want to read and focus without any distractions. I don't know many of the regulars there.

Likewise, I sometimes go to the Starbucks in Newton Lower Falls. This is a great centrally located spot when I have to meet new clients who don't know the Needham area. I also frequently stop there following nearby doctor's appointments at Newton Wellesley Hospital, particularly when I have had to fast for blood work. This will be my treat after a pre-visit fast.

Another location I frequent is on Needham Street in Newton near the bathroom design store, Splash. This Starbucks was remodeled a year or so ago and has nice areas to sit both inside and outside, as well as designer bathrooms.

For a change of pace I will occasionally visit **Café Nero** in Wellesley or in Dedham. They have very good coffee, great pastries, and comfortable seating. Since I just about know everyone at my local Starbucks, this is a good meeting place if I want to be a bit more incognito.

I have to admit that I was never a Dunkin' Donuts person, but since they introduced the Dark Roast blend in 2014[20] I have given them a second chance. I do like their dark roast hot and iced coffee and even enjoy their lattes. I have even downloaded the Dunkin' App on my phone. Although not my top destination of choice, Dunkin' is a welcome stop when highway driving. They offer a consistent and reasonably priced drink option.

Lastly, and going full circle, I would be remiss to not mention that after many years and since selling the Coffee Connection to Starbucks, in 2012 George Howell founded **George Howell Coffee,** featuring specialty coffee. The first location opened on Walnut Street in Newtonville near where it all began.[21] George Howell has since expanded his operations to include six locations. Each shop features a café, and some have space for specialty brewing classes. Although I no longer live in Newtonville, I do stop by for a cup of brew whenever I am in the area.

Sign in front of George Howell Coffee shop

To this day, coffee is my thing. On a rare occasion I will get Bruce to stop with me to get a cup, but he is still not one to linger. He does enjoy the fruits of my labor and will welcome a Frappuccino or Caramel Macchiato as a take-home treat using my accumulated reward points. I work diligently to accrue these and since I don't drink much besides regular coffee, I use these as treats for family members.

Since the start of the pandemic, my favorite café has become my home. Morning starts with a French dark roast, and then I sometimes treat myself to an afternoon cappuccino.

Part Five:
2020—The New Normal
of "Covid Coffee"

Virtual Coffee

Long before the COVID-19 pandemic I had virtual coffees with family and friends. I used to coordinate coffee time with my mom while she was in Florida. She would go to the nearby Starbucks in Palm Harbor and I would simultaneously visit my local Starbucks. We would call each other and chat about the kids, life, weather, and more. This was a time devoted to focused conversation over a cup of coffee and reminiscent of my childhood days with Mom, Grandma, and Aunt Elaine.

I also would sometimes FaceTime friends while sitting outside where privacy wasn't an issue or use Starbucks as my virtual office when I had busy work to do.

Never did I envision this becoming the standard way to meet clients and friends. Then the pandemic hit.

It's Zoom Café Time

Since the COVID pandemic mandated stay-at-home orders last spring, we have had to learn to live under a "new normal." I now start my day with a cup of coffee while I read the paper and check my social media.

I thought I would really miss my daily visits to coffee shops, but honestly, I have come to enjoy making coffee at home and having some time to spend doing things around the house.

The first few weeks took a bit of adjustment. To keep my mind busy, I started taking a series of selfie photos going through all my collected coffee mugs from the various Starbucks I had visited. I posted many of these on Instagram with the hashtag **#starbucksathomewhilesocialdistancing** and **#coffeeathomewhilesocialdistancing.** These images are scattered throughout this book. Coincidentally, since I started writing this book, Starbucks has created a series of virtual backgrounds for customers to use when having their coffee at home. If interested, you can use these as your Zoom background to feel the Starbucks vibe.[22]

I have since been busy almost every day with online training to learn how to conduct my real estate business virtually to better serve my clients' needs. I now brew a pot to enjoy during these classes. In addition, I have had many meetings using Zoom, Microsoft Teams, or other meeting apps.

I have also attended a few virtual networking coffee events, including some hosted by **Improv Andy/Andrew Winig.** He has focused his events on how to connect initially via a coffee meeting. I credit this program as the prompt to start penning this book. (*I had met Improv Andy/Andy Winig at a Newton Needham Chamber of Commerce networking event pre-pandemic.*)[23]

Under the old normal whenever I had a new real estate client, I would meet them in person before starting their search. Pre-pandemic, I often chose Starbucks as a neutral place to chat to learn basic information about the client's property needs. As mentioned, I have found that an initial coffee meetup is often a great way to have an introductory conversation. Chatting over coffee gives each party a safe space to comfortably get to know each other. This has since migrated to virtual meetings using Zoom or FaceTime platforms.

As home has become my office during COVID, I have daily Zoom and social meetings where we all share a cup of coffee while chatting. I have even upgraded to the professional-level unlimited Zoom account.

On a daily basis my go-to brew is French Roast.[24] Sometimes for diversion I will make a pour-over coffee or a cappuccino with a frother. As I was learning to adapt to home brewing, my brother-in-law Donald also shared a great method to make cold brew. This can be found in the supplemental recipe section, in the back of the book.

On the Personal Side of My New Normal Routine

Again, as written elsewhere my one constant daily norm is my "cup of Joe." Through it all, I start each day with this ritual. The only thing that has changed in all these years of coffee consumption is the ratio of coffee to milk. I now drink primarily black coffee unless I am having a specialty drink.

I have been doing intermittent fasting for a little over a year now and thus usually don't eat until at least noon. Of note, I typically eat within an 8-hour window each day. Black coffee is permitted during the fast time, as milk triggers higher sugar levels. Whenever I get a hunger pang, sipping black coffee holds my appetite off.

I try to do yoga or other exercises around 11 each day and then have lunch around noon. I am often on the same cup of coffee and can microwave to reheat it.

After lunch I generally have more meetings or I will go out to do a few things. I often take a long mid-afternoon walk and will sometimes have a cold brew or a cappuccino upon my return later in the afternoon. Sometimes I will drink this afternoon coffee while having a social Zoom or FaceTime with family and friends.

Closing Remarks

Although much of my daily routine has changed since the pandemic hit, Starbucks has remained a constant in my life. I can't even begin to count the number of times I have been to Starbucks. If I calculate over the course of 30 years at even four times a week this would be about 210 visits a year and close to 6000 lifetime visits. It's been said that doing anything for 21 days forms a habit, so Starbucks coffee must be part of my bloodline now.

As I have spent more time at home since the pandemic, I have learned that I don't need to visit Starbucks every day. I can enjoy coffee in the comfort of my home.

One of the greatest gifts from the pandemic has been the opportunity to write this book. As you have seen, my life has been like a puzzle with many different parts. The common thread tying these together has been the one constant of coffee. My other passions of talking with others, reading books, traveling, and theater share a few similarities. Each of these are portals into another's personal experiences. As I journey through life, I am an explorer. I am always interested in meeting new people and discovering what makes people tick. I recently heard an interview where Sean Penn told Howard Stern that life's greatest freedom is the ability to explore one's curiosities. I believe this is true. Coffee has been my partner on many of these adventures.

To this day I continue to love coffee. It keeps me grounded, provides comfort, and will be with me no matter where I live. I am thankful for that, and although the medium changes I always look forward to my next cup of coffee and the opportunity to make a new coffee connection.

Dear Coffee-Connectees (if you made it this far, you are part of this group),

I hope you now understand more about my coffee connections and what has driven me to "drink." When I read the book Midlife: A Philosophical Guide, *I reflected on the different approaches we each take to life. While many enjoy the "atelic" process of sitting and slowly sipping our coffee, others prefer the "telic" approach of drinking it quickly before tackling the next project.*

As you may have noted throughout this book, I use each cup as an opportunity to learn a bit more about life and to observe my surroundings. Whether listening to one's conversations, reading, or meeting a new person, I take the time to enjoy each sip. Starbucks has often been a safe space to explore the world around me without feeling the need to constantly have a defined agenda.

I have now come to understand that opposites attract, and perhaps this yin and yang is often the key to successful relationships. While I may sit back and philosophize, one may be working hard to provide for their personal and family needs. I appreciate this with much gratitude, but I also hope each reader will be able to learn the importance of balance and take time to slow down and sip your daily brew.

Wendy

Add-ons: All Fun Places Have a Gift Shop at the End

Je Me Souviens?

Just about everyone knows I love Starbucks and coffee, and many of my friends and family members excitedly bring me Starbucks items or coffee-related souvenirs from their travels.

In addition, I enjoy collecting Starbucks mugs at each new destination I visit, and as such it has become a great way to reflect on my trip after returning home. Some of my favorite mugs include those from Hawaii, Barcelona, Miami, Las Vegas, New York (I have several), San Francisco, London, and Prague. I rotate through these to reminisce about my past travels. As mentioned previously, at the start of the pandemic I did my own "tour de Java" in my kitchen, posting an Instagram selfie each day posing with a different mug from a location I had visited. You can see these photos on Instagram: **#starbucksathomewhilesocialdistancing** or **#coffeeathomewhilesocialdistancing**.

I have received a few other Starbucks mugs through the years as birthday gifts and always appreciate a new one for my collection.

Beth (a friend I often meet for coffee) also gave me a coffee-cup-shaped hot plate as a birthday gift.

A few of my favorite stories about other acquisitions include a coffee mug from **Aroma** in Israel. When my daughter Michelle went on Birthrite a few years ago, she wanted to bring me a gift from Aroma. She asked if she could buy a mug at one of their cafés and was told that they didn't sell them. She really wanted one and told the barista how much her mother loves Aroma. He gave her one to sneak out of the café and bring home. I am probably one of the few Americans now with an Aroma mug. On a subsequent trip to Japan, Michelle also brought me a Starbucks Japan mug. How cool is that?

Rachael was in DC visiting my niece, Samantha, a few years ago and found a great framed photo/print from a street vendor titled "Wake-up Washington DC." She saw it and said, "It's so Mom" and had to buy it for me. This title is still quite true to this day. She also bought me a great mug in early 2020 when visiting Lake Tahoe.

My brother Max found an amazing mug with a photo of a person sitting by the dock of the bay with her dog that could be custom ordered; thus, he surprised me with a "Wendy and Delilah" version. It is perfect for Cape Cod and off season to think about my summer visits.

On the flip side, when Greg started NYU one of the first things I bought him was a Boston Starbucks mug to keep in his dorm as a subtle reminder that "There is no place like home." He has been home with me since the onset of the pandemic, and I have reclaimed that mug for my collection.

Housewarming Gifts to Myself

2005

Starbucks sold their own coffee brewer up until about 2010. We moved from our raised ranch to a new house in 2005 with all stainless-steel appliances. The Starbucks Barista Coffee Maker was the same brushed stainless steel and I bought one as a housewarming gift to myself. This was the first item in our new kitchen. Our move took us to a different part of the same town, and thus I was able to bring most of my kitchen items to the new house, including the "Tour de Java" poster, to be fully functional on actual move-in day. I added a few plaques, "Café" and "Bistro," to complete the decor.

2014

Likewise, whenever I move now the coffee maker is the first item on the packing list. We bought a Cape Cod house about five years ago, and before moving in I stocked up on coffee, wine, and ice cream. These are now my three staples wherever I live. Instead of "Coffee, Tea, or Me," my MO is "Coffee, Wine, or Ice Cream." I love entertaining and know from experience that my guests, no matter what age, will enjoy one of the three, or maybe all and in different orders depending on how long they are visiting.

The Right Tools for Making Coffee

I had my Starbucks Barista machine for about five years until it died and believe it was discontinued. As I was researching replacements, my brother Max encouraged me to learn how to make pour-over coffee. Max is an avid pour-over maker, and he provided complete instructions on which one to buy and how to make it. I have perfected this art and now enjoy a pour-over as an afternoon treat. I ended up buying the **Cuisinart Extreme Brew,** which I love, and it is a great way to make a pot of coffee. I really like my coffee to be hot, so in general I do prefer using this to the pour-over method. In addition, I like to measure 5 to 6 cups so I can have refills. Coffee is much better and fresher if freshly ground; thus, I buy whole beans and grind them daily on a medium grind. When possible, I buy French Roast in 2½-lb bags at Costco. During the pandemic I have been going through a bag a month.

I use a **Cuisinart Supreme Coffee Grinder** that adjusts for grind level. I do a medium grind, generally equivalent to a #4 if I order it ground at Starbucks. I also have a **Krupps Fast Touch Coffee Grinder** as a backup.

My mom was very perceptive and knew a deep secret about our marriage that we had kept hidden from most of our mutual friends. While I loved coffee, Bruce did not, and he only drank it to stay awake. In addition, Bruce only drank flavored coffee to hide the taste. I am a traditionalist. Mom bought us a **Keurig** as an anniversary gift thinking this would allow Bruce to have flavored coffee he could enjoy. He could now brew a quick cup of Hazelnut or Vanilla Caramel while I still had my French Roast. I personally prefer the Cuisinart, but the Keurig is a great way to make a quick cup. I bought a reusable adapter to brew Starbucks coffee using the Keurig and occasionally will do this if pressed for time.

For pour-over, I use a **Hario 4-cup glass beaker** (as recommended by Max) and nonbleached filters. I will share the recipe in the appendix.

After owning a few different cappuccino makers that ended up breaking after a year or so, I now brew my coffee and use a coffee press (also Max's recommendation) to froth my foam. This is the easiest foolproof method. See the appendix for the recipe. I recently bought a **NORPRO** press for the froth.

Lastly, I also make cold brew with my Cuisinart coffee maker.

Appendix: Recipes

Traditional Brew

I use 1 coffee scoop per 1 cup measure of water for regular coffee. French Roast is great for daily coffee.

I use a Cuisinart Extreme Brew, but this can also be made in a French Press or any basic coffee maker.

Occasionally, if I want a stronger espresso type for a cappuccino I will add an extra 1–2 scoops of coffee to the water measure.

Cold Brew

To make cold brew, I add 2-3 extra scoops to a pot of brewed coffee. If the coffee maker brews 12 cups, I add 14-15 scoops of coffee and brew as usual. I let the coffee cool for a few hours and then pour it in a bottle to refrigerate overnight. It comes out great.

Cappuccino

Sometimes I want an afternoon cappuccino and will use 1-2 cups from the cold brew when freshly brewed (above) as the coffee.

I put 1-2 oz. of milk in a frother and pump it for 30-50 seconds until it creates a froth. Let it settle and microwave it for 30 seconds. Then pour the froth over the coffee. I add a sprinkle of cinnamon or chocolate for flavor.

Pour-Over[25]

STEP 1: Measure and grind coffee. Use the designated pour-over coffee measuring spoon and Hario filter.

STEP 2: Pour hot water through the filter to wet the paper and to warm up the filter and the cup or decanter.

STEP 3: Add the ground coffee to the filter and tamp it down to be flat. Measure one full scoop of coffee to one coffee cup measure in the carafe.

STEP 4: Wet the ground coffee all around. Let stand for 30-45 seconds.

STEP 5: Pour more water with a rotating movement on the grounds. Make sure that all the coffee grounds are wet by moving in a circular motion. You DO NOT want to create a funnel. Ideally, the ground coffee will look almost like a mushroom and be wet evenly, with the water flowing through all of the coffee. Keep going until close to your desired cup measure.

STEP 6: Use the rest of the water to slowly clean up the brim of the filter and again continue to pour remaining needed water on the grounds with a rotating movement until the number of cups in the carafe equals the coffee scoop measure.

STEP 7: Swirl the cup or decanter before serving, then enjoy!

Epilogue

I started conceptualizing this book more than ten years ago. I took notes and pulled outlines together from several starting points until finally putting pen to paper this past spring during the pandemic lockdowns. Thus, I have called this book my COVID Project. In addition to this project, while writing this book, I simultaneously began to volunteer on the 2020 Presidential Campaign. Every morning, with a cup of home-brewed coffee in hand, I soon found myself splitting my time between the two.

Writing has always been a form of relaxation and stress relief for me. I have relished the time spent over these past several months reminiscing about shared coffees and conversations with family and friends.

Mid-summer I bought a coffee mug with the logo "America Needs A Big Cup of Joe." How appropriate for my life! With gratitude I hope that my volunteer efforts made a small contribution to the 2020 election results. This point in time became special for one more reason. Since election day I finalized and signed the contract with Lisa Pelto, my publisher from Concierge Marketing, to bring this book to print. I am very excited to be able to share my end product with you. After reading this book, I hope you will take the time to treat yourself to your favorite version of a cup of Joe!

Acknowledgments: Thank You to My "Coffee-Mates"

Thank you to my family and friends for encouraging me to write this book and for becoming important lifelong connections throughout this journey.

I have had many "coffee-mates" along the way and have visited Starbucks at least 6000 times since they opened more than 25 years ago. Although it would be nearly impossible to recount every coffee memory, I have grown with each and every encounter and conversation I have had while sharing a cup of coffee. I would like to recognize my frequent friendly "sippers" – Joan R. in the early Coffee Connection years, and Beth B., Beth D., Midge D., Wendy M., Ricki L., Jayne R. and many others during the latter ones. Thank you to my special family and close to-family friends Karen J., Joyce J. and Julie G. for our extended birthday lunches always topped off with a Starbucks coffee.

A big thank you to my friend Rob Brandt for being late for a coffee meeting thus enabling me to find my dog, Delilah while waiting. I thank Keith Greenfield for helping me catch the theater bug and everyone I worked with during my "production" years with Open Fields, the Dover Foundation, FOPA, and Temple Aliyah. In particular, thank you to my production team coffee buddies, Ruth Townsend and Lisa Kane for always insisting we meet at Starbucks. Thank you to everyone I met during the Sloan Fellows year for allowing me to share and become "the local one".

On the professional side thank you to my early mentors at Emhart, Dun and Bradstreet Corporation and McCormack & Dodge. Wearing my Realtor hat, thank you to my Hammond and Coldwell Banker colleagues and especially my administrative support staff who always covered the phones when I snuck out to grab a coffee. I also wish to thank the Newton Needham Chamber of Commerce for enabling my networking passion.

Thank you to Arthur Tsicoulias for being my freelance photographer. Thank you to Bruce Reinstein for sharing publishing advice. Thank you to George Howell for conceptualizing and introducing me to my first coffee connections. Thank you to Michael King for inspiring me to become an author, Andy Winig for helping me launch this project, and Kevin Walsh for advising me on how to publish a book. After Kevin's referral, thank you to Lisa Pelto, Ellie Godwin, Janet Tilden and the team for working with me to actually publish this book.

Thank you to childhood friends Marcy S., Nancy G., Tobi W., Debbie P., and Jo R. who have joined with me since the early years of sleepovers, dating, and then as coffee connections during all phases in my explorations. Jo has also become a "client for life" since my real estate launch.

Again thank you to my sister in law, Karen who will meet me whenever she is free, her husband Donald who taught me how to make Cold Brew coffee, as well as Samantha and Jessie who always shared Starbucks adventures (sometimes before Hebrew School) with my kids growing up. Thank you to sister in law, Linda, who also made Starbucks an important stop on every journey and my In-Laws Amalia and Joe who always supported my frequent habit of wanting a cup of "Joe".

Thank you to our exchange students Samuele Barin and Naomi Fueri for teaching me about European Café Culture. Thank you to my close family friends, the Weinsteins, and cousins, The Levis, who I have met along the way on many travel ventures.

Thank you to my Mom for introducing me to coffee, my Dad for his coffee inspiring conversations and my brother Max for teaching me the Art of Pour-over and Dry Cappuccinos. Thank you to Vered, his wife, and Keren, Eric, and Shira who spent hours with me at Starbucks during cheer practices and while at Camp Bornstein. Lastly thank you to Delilah for being my partner on many coffee walks and to my immediate family Bruce, Greg, Rachael, and Michelle for learning to acquire a taste for good coffee and being a big part of my journey.

Endnotes

1. https://www.ncausa.org/About-Coffee/What-is-Coffee

2. https://en.wikipedia.org/wiki/Maxwell_House_Haggadah

3. *Coffee, Tea or Me?* [20th printing, 1969] (The uninhibited memoirs of two airline stewardesses: Here's the real low-down on the high-flying stewardess scene...) Mass Market Paperback – January 1, 1969

4. https://en.wikipedia.org/wiki/Saturday_Night_Fever

5. https://pubmed.ncbi.nlm.nih.gov/6521479/

6. https://www.boston.com/culture/health/2014/07/17/why-21-a-look-at-our-nations-drinking-age

7. George Howell Coffee | George Howell Coffee website

    George Howell (entrepreneur) – Wikipedia

    https://www.bostonmagazine.com/2012/11/27/george-howell-coffee-connection-starbucks/

8. https://www.nytimes.com/1976/08/31/archives/you-cant-judge-a-bagel-by-the-decor-around-it.html

9. https://youtu.be/le1QF3uoQNg

10. https://en.wikipedia.org/wiki/Peter_principle

11. "All Coffee Connections Will Become Starbucks" by Nelson C. Hsu January 19, 1996 issue of The Harvard Crimson

12. "What Cafés Did for Liberalism" by Adam Gopnik

13. https://www.open-fields.info

14. http://www.starbucksmelody.com/2013/12/20/the-star-bucks-card-2001-2013-then-and-now/

15. *Pour Your Heart Into It: How Starbucks Built a Company One Cup at a Time* by Howard Schultz. Hachette Books, 1999.

16. *The Greening of America by Charles Reich.* Published in 1970.

17. *Why I Read Non-Fiction,* Episode 7; https://podcasts.apple.com/us/podcast/there-were-10-000-books-with-wendy-bornstein/id1460758183?i=1000440442660

18. *Midlife: A Philosophical Guide* by Kieran Setiya. Princeton University Press, 2017.

19. *Crucial Conversations: Tools for Talking When Stakes Are High,* Second Edition, by Kerry Patterson, Joseph Grenny, et al.

20. https://news.dunkindonuts.com/news/dunkin-donuts-debuts-a-bold-new-brew-with-rainforest-alliance-certi-fiedTM-dark-roast-coffee

21. https://www.georgehowellcoffee.com/newtonville-cafe/

    https://www.georgehowellcoffee.com/knowledge/notes-from-george/

22. https://stories.starbucks.com/stories/2020/you-can-still-work-from-starbucks-with-virtual-backgrounds/

23. https://improvandy.com

24. Starbucks has stopped carrying French Roast at their stores, and you can only purchase it online or at the supermarket. I don't quite understand the logic of this. Costco members can buy 2½-lb. bags.

25. https://www.baristainstitute.com/brewguides-2/hario-v60

About the Author

Wendy is a Realtor with Coldwell Banker and an active member of her local community. Her greatest passion is connecting people with the right resources to meet their needs, whether their needs are personal or business related. In her free time, she loves to read, write, explore the arts, travel, cook… and of course, meet friends for coffee.

She welcomes you to become her next coffee connection. Please follow her on Instagram @WendyBWrites or by email at wsbornstein@gmail.com.

Made in United States
North Haven, CT
17 January 2023